Inspirational Collective Poetry

"The Writing That Heals"

BOOK 2

"The Tragedy in a Tangled Talented Mind"

Poems by Q. M. Malinga

Inspirational Collective Poetry
"The Writing That Heals"
C/o Hlalanathi Community Theatre Project
P.O. Box 7508, Johannesburg 2000, South Africa

Tel/Fax
+27 11 725 5413

Mobile
+27 72 715 9798

E-mail
Inspcol2@hotmail.com
or
qhubani_marvellous_m@hotmail.com

ISBN: **978-1-910115-29-9**

Prepared for publication by LionheART Publishing House

INTRODUCTION

"Because I know where I come from, I as well know where I am going to."

The Tragedy in a Tangled Talented Mind is the second book of **Inspirational Collective Poetry** by **Qhubani M. Malinga**.

This writing and publishing did not just happen only for the love of it but as inspiration from which the name came about. After having been involved in the arts industry for many years as a stage-performing artist, I have hardly ever expressed or revealed my feelings. This book is for other people who find it very hard to express themselves through talking.

With this writing I hope to reach out to the unreachable through the stage.

Because these poems are based on reality, please don't feel offended but be challenged into transformation to a positive attitude or behavior towards people. I am not using these poems to either protest or rebel against anyone above, behind or besides me. I am not a rival and strongly combat all the deprivation and demoralization that I'm going through in this struggle. Hence, I advise my fellow comrades in, or still to join, the struggle, about all its ups and downs. Forewarned is forearmed; be positively inspired as you read through this book.

I voice some phenomenal facts that me, myself and I encounter on a day-to-day basis, not outrageously but philosophically in this mysterious challenging artistic life in which I live. I urge you to begin to make a positive move that will bring about a revolutionary change in your society rather than sitting back and doing nothing or pointing fingers at others who do nothing.

If ever you are with me in the struggle, keep calculating your steps. If you know where you come from, you will know where you want to go. If you believe in yourself, just look around and see the vast fortune that you have.

ACKOWLEDGEMENTS

The Creator of Heaven and Earth, home to all the living and dead. I hope this is also a great contribution toward His Gospel. I believe He has created and put us on to this earth with different purposes, therefore this is the work that He has anointed me to do for his people.

I greatly honor all those that have allowed the Devil to use them to become obstacles to my life. *"Without you I would not have been inspired to write these poems and I hope they will help all of us to understand each other rather than being tiresome toward one another. I declare heroism to you for all the hostility you have shown towards each and every goal that I have set up for myself. It has strengthened me up to this point; surely without you I would not have written anything."*

My family members, who have always been with me in all different kinds of situations. *Not too far but too soon we will be celebrating my success in this struggle that has almost separated us.*

The nations that are striving to make a living through arts, this stands not only for me but also for all of us. *This is how I remember all the mystical power of your good works all over the world.*

To all these specific individuals, schools and organizations: Hlalanathi Community Theatre Project, M.U.K.A. (Most United Knowledgeable Artist) project, Revolutionary Productions, Korth family, Elizabeth, Michelle Barrow for grooming me, David Epstein and Basa Tutorial Institute,

Josef Glosner and Gymnasium Parsberg, Germany, Andreas Knudel and the Dalka family. I will be able to stand and celebrate victory through the support that has come from you in different forms. You are not forgotten, all my friends and well-wishers around the world; I cannot mention and finish all the names, may your lives be filled with more blessings as you enjoy your read.

CONTENTS

The Tragedy in a Tangled Talented Mind

POOR ME IN A RICH WORLD

It's my calmness and consciousness
That I give to their feelings
I have humbled myself because I care
Love and logical mind
I offer myself to any request

I cater and care for the careless
Standing in the middle of the bushy thorns
Withstanding and understanding
The strong prevailing winds
Threatening to blow me away
Instead I let them carry along my messages
To both the poor and the rich

Because I do not just stand
I stand still and stupidly
Standing to save the survivors
Awaiting for those massive scolds
To diss my efforts but failing
And I shall stand still.

TILL I DIE

I swear not swearing
But it is mine till I kiss goodbye to this earth
Born with it
Right in me
Lived with it
Still in me even now
Because it is mine

I never picked it up from streets
I shall journey with it
So as it will remain in me
With it right in my soul

I may cry for the land or wealth
Just like many nations have cried
Not for the riches in my mind
Thus my mobile property
My gift, talent and intellectuality
That I will never lose.

MY SUCCESS

This is a competitive world
That needs great soldiers
That has gone through the jungles
Think and rethink what you have thought
Having great thoughts and force
To recall your mind considerately
Reviving the lost hope

The cruel and envious rivals
End up killing the innocent
To gain success and survival
Being too envious
Yet not ambitious

The envious are always anxious
To those living simply but successfully
Let everyone now read from me
In all that I have desired

Mine will come through my strength
Mostly strengthened by my non-rivalry
Not in any means shall I concede
Challenges to let me down
But they will strengthen me too.

GLITTERING SWORD

It is better to be good
Than wanting to be good
One should consider being good
For only being good

Good men humble themselves
Sometimes being scolded
Not for goodness' sake
Nor because of stupidity
But for the respect that everyone deserves
Moreover for life experiences

Wanting to be good
Leads to the loss of some good experiences
And results in foolishness
Through the fooling and under-looking
Hence undermining the intellectuality

Good friends need to be considerate
To care for each other's feelings
Accept wrongness when necessary
Good friendship needs no pretense
For the sharpness of a glittering sword
Has always been dangerous

EVERY DAY WITH EVERY NIGHT

Why is it that the sun rises and sets?
Why does it have to rise?
If it will then set?
Why is it said to be stationary?
While it is set to rising and setting

One might think it sets
Because we need to rest at night
Sleeping as common everywhere
Geographical and scientifically
It is stationary
Only the earth is rotating

Has this got the same meaning to me?
Generation of energy on its light
Means giving power to me
For generation and digestion

When it rises I wake up
To appreciate what it has for me
My goals, facing my challenges

When it sets I sleep not rest
But start visualizing my visions
Striving to make them count and real
With every day and night of no rest

CRYING WON'T HELP

The universe was created
With many different challenges
To be faced by me and you
Tackled by both of us

Achievers have once or twice lost
But never stopped achieving hope
Though not ideal to encourage
It is a necessary challenge
To learn through mistakes

Sit but not back in life
And never fail before trying
Weep no tears
That will mean no nothing
Except inner feelings

When obstructed
Weep no tears
But strive to keep on trying
And cheer yourself up
You will be an achiever

MY DEVOTION

Despite despise and deprivation
Detested and discriminated
Distorted or destructed
Derided and discriminated
Disturbed and depressed
Discrete and discouraged
Never shall I get despondent

Despite despair and destitution
Devil decoyed and detained
Deterred or detached
Deserted and diminished
Set up in dilemma
Dictated and diddled
Never shall I be despondent

Already been destined
To all visions in life
Never shall I allow devaluation
Never shall I be devastated
Neither discredited nor discarded
Never shall I discreet
For I am dedicated and determined.

SHOULD I FORGET

Why, repeatedly why should I?
A spark that sparkled into real light
Ruled into my now promising life
Fire that I must keep burning
Will burn till I die
Should I forget then?

Not at all
And again why?
I would love to remember
The deprivation and suppression
Sanctioned and perturbed
Forced to perversely live
Scolded now and then
And I would love to remember

In my contemplations
Shall remain the old past days
Always perpetrated and saddened
Times rolling on my integrity
While known to disintegrate

But all that I complimented
Comprehended in my rich mind
And I have forgiven
But I would love to remember

FORGIVEN

Forgiving you
Is not forgetting you
Neither forgetting your wrongs
Because forgiving is not forgetting
But is only forgiving

It is out of wrong
That you can correct
For you cannot correct the correct
But only the incorrect
A sorry with positive change
Or, with no positive action
Equal to no sorry

It's out of forgiving and forgetting
That the same wrong can be done
Knowing the wrong being done
Is knowing the wrong done before
Then forgive but not forget

TIMES

Down below the earth
Are my riches
Moving towards prosperity
Means stepping on my riches
Hence kicking some of them away
Though remarkable is not my question

But how then will I prosper?
When walking on my riches
Sounding really weird
Are my thoughts of getting under the earth
Because by then I will be dead
And I will not come back

Can the dead not bring them up?
Must I dig a pit from where I stand?
Yes I can get my riches
But with no more way towards my prosperity

DESERTED

Oh! What a devaluation of life
A fall from no force of gravity
It cannot be
That I stand truly like this

My life was once thriving
Love, peace and joy spilling
Out of my heart and all over
In the now empty soul of my heart
I wonder if I have to believe it

I would let the good times roll
Chilling out with "amagang"
Buzzing with "abobaby"
Filling up the table
Brown, blue, green and everything
Just none's business

I wonder if I ever made friends
Or money made friends for me
But money has bought poverty for me
Not even a fly bothers to visit me
Because I have died while still breathing
With no smell that can bring closer the flies
Gone are those good times that rolled
Gone are "amajents nobaby abamoja"

UNEXPECTED BLOWS

Pity this world is
I do not know what it is
Neither what to do
Should I beg for any mercy?
And from whom should I beg?
Why should I beg anywhere?

And if I have to
I must say to God
Please have mercy on me
Not to this earth
Even to the merciful
But to those that do not have

Unexpected blows come from all over
Intending to harm my body
Targeting all the strongest points in me
Mostly from contemplated fondest friends
Varying variously from various faces

I still stand firmly in the middle
With no reason to beg for their mercy
Because they do not have any
And surely they do not have

OFTEN VIOLENT

It is but a shame
A very big sorrow
Renouncing the good hope I had
What hell of a shame it is

The unpronounced facts on this earth
Have denounced the good hope I had
A non-violent but peaceful life
Dilapidated the gift of love I had
To share with the loving

I have become an alien man to this world
The sadists celebrate their victory
While I drown in the unworthy repentance
Shedding tears from my hurt emotional feelings
That deprives chance for my love
Weeping on my profusely bleeding wounds
Deep down in my heart
Forcing me not to care for none

IN THE BEACH

While summer time brings about happy hours
People get time to be on good holidays
Visit and disperse on the beach
Like a lost herd of cattle
Grazing in no-grazing land

The lazy fox gives excuses
Likewise and always wanting a rest
Tiring selves form no tiredness
Resting endless and restless rests

Some even forgetting who they are
What is around them
They lie naked
Thinking that they were born naked
So they have the right as humanity
So let them be as they think

MOTHER

The world at large grows
Salutes and honors you, Mother
Indeed deserving the honor
Talking not only to you, Mother
But to you, Mother
Do you value this great honor?
If so, then this question is for you

Mother, yes you Mother
Not with an offending will
Let me pause a silly
But so dated with facts question
And never mind answering
Though I desperately need the answer
But only for you, Mother

What does the answer mean to you?
As well remaining yours
Mother, what makes you mother?
And I will only honor the answering
For you are really honorable

LOVE SLAVE

Love is a big necessity of life
Though a big challenge of all
It needs commitment
Combined with great compassion
With a double cheer coincidence

Despite its phenomenal fact
That says it is blind
One needs to remain vigilant
Because it may well turn into slavery

Pity is the one with too much love
For there lies a big risk of slavery
Caused by the love abusers
Who never consider its necessity
Denouncing pity and mercy
To the ones they think they love

Let not yourself suffer
Suffering from love slavery
Through inconsiderate feelings
With infinite and inevitable love giving
Forgetting to calculate the return love
The necessity is to love
And be loved as well in return
In the same measure you give

LOVE AND SEX

Both Jenny and Jack give it time
Jack's joke is mostly sex
While Jenny journeys for love
And never confuses the two
Yet Jack concludes and confuses

Well of course
Where there is no love
There should not be any sex
For it may badly turn out

Jack tends to give an excuse of last
Anyhow, what is it?
Called a lust
Where does it come from?
Does it exist to no relationship?
Oh! What a complication.

Only not a complication
If sex could be considered
Only as a result of love
And not as love or lust
Because love is a passion
Which may lead to sex

REVOLUTIONARY SON

Down below the earth
Where my destination is

Only when I get there
I will be declared heroic

Yet I maneuver now
For a dramatic change in the poor

It is when I die
When my judges will discover their wrong

Having no time of avenging on me
Nor rebuking my undiplomatic say

Let them stop chattering around
And have the freedom to come straight to me

As there will be no time when I die
Yet in no revolution

Never mind about my wrong sometimes
For I do not mean to hurt or hate

But there are just common mistakes
That I am not common with

Only pick them up
For your positive and dramatic change

MORE THAN A WARLORD

Here and there
Stands a nobleman
Of less nonentity by appearance

The marginalized man
Who has never been eradicated
By being magnificent

Of course more than a warlord
Unlike the warlike
Never bothering other man's life

The explosive in explicit
Fearing none dilemma
But bravely voicing

Despite vulnerability
And the exclusion
Has philosophically tolerated mankind

WAR OF THE JUNGLE

In the tangled talents many are found
Interrogated and discovered
And many are to be

Heads that smashed co-operatively
Rejoicing with their talents
Not considering a market out of them

Are now smashing rudely and puzzled
In the now tangled scramble for survival
Being politicized

The now war of the jungle
Survival of the fittest
The rebellion of talents

Where legends have become rivals
Rivalry reviving for survival
With the now scrambling new generation

PIECES OF STONES

Take a look at them
They are just pieces of stones
That surely cannot move
Except when picked up
And thrown to another point

Forgetting only one vital point
That they only remain useless
If you think so
And do not make use of them

You pick them up
Where they are naturally grounded
And preserving the soil
You make them useless

And if you think they are useless
Just let them remain grounded
And the soil will remain preserved
Otherwise you will see their usefulness
When they are already finished

IN JUVENILE

Hollywood of the holy
Home of the survivors
Home of rejoicing
A place of great awareness
A place of junior correction

Where torture turns a good thing
Skills develop more
The way paved for the blind
And for the intelligence abusers
Yet too foolish to even fool the fools

The place accommodates you
Even if it is hard to accept it
Moreover
Your passion live you
To live with the live
In a very good future

IF IT'S ME

When I am treated inhumanly
Disrespected and disappointed
I have to accept

If you are treated
Equally and important
You deviate and get upset

When it's you and me
I must compromise
While you seek sympathy

Why seek sympathy
When not pathetic
But paramount?

I will of course compromise
Because I am non-competent
But very much confident

DIFFERENCES

Our differences are not determination
To judgment of one another
Neither inferiority nor sabotage
To anyone's passion

Be in our color or complexion
Our religion or culture
What we
Or how we do
Likes and dislikes

We are born different
We need proper calculation
To our differences
As they determine
Compound compositions

DREAMING OF AFRICAN CULTURE

Once more again my motherland
Just as life showed up before
Still shines ever more
More brighter than ever before

Twilight was predicted for the 20th century
With only the vanishing environments
The life was thriving
In the now empty soils of Africa

But I still stand to say
Live is thriving more lively
In the inherit aged Mother Africa
With its cultural property

If evolution and revolution once existed
They still exist even today
And shall exist for ever
And shall rejoice, cultural contented Africa

The conspiracies
Shall become conspicuous
Africa shall see the marginalized
Succeeding socially and economically

IN STRUGGLE

The late legends always wiped tears
Tied up their shoelaces
Intending to rise up and fight
Strong blows from their mouths unblocked
But entertaining and alerting
Hence bring about revolution

Called legend yet still in struggle
Still voicing from the backyards
Urging me, myself and I to rise up

Admitting but not regretting
The sorry they started
They still inspire self and I
Blossoming just as before

They tried and failed
But never failed blossoming
With the mere mercy of great merits
Already the told stories
In the arts struggle

MISJUDGED

My judges and prosecutors
My detectives
My self-proclaimed lords
Together with your envious shepherd

I hereby forward this earnest request
Standing beside myself
Living locomotive
A lawyer of my own
Standing not to beg for any mercy
Because you are not merciful either

You're being judgmental to me
Have misjudged me

You fail to mend your own wagons
And carry to the limelight
Your monotonous instruments
That you foolishly impress
By being merely cowardly to me

Truly expressing myself
Not in vanity but with sanity
I will maneuver

My tranquility is not inflexible
Nor letting any transfixion
Not even making me a culprit
So get me right and realistic

CELEBRATING MY DEATHDAY

Thank you Lord for all the nasty
Who celebrated my birthday
Together with the good
And with all the best wishers

To all the nasty
Jealous, evil, envious and anxious
Not with any offending mind
Never mind my death

For I will be there again
Celebrating together with you
As that is the only day
You are eagerly waiting to celebrate

You do not want to celebrate
My thriving life
But well wishing
For a short, a safe journey
Down below the earth

STILL YOU MY MOTHER

Will I be wrong to say?
It is of no use saying sorry to you
No reason to ask for a welcome back home

Ask me not why you know
Knowing because of your feelings
I only have to thank you, Mother

Without any note or goodbye
I jetted far away from home
But thank you that you have been my mother

I quietly demanded what you did not have
Then blamed you with irresponsibility
But still you were my mother

I never understood your suffering
Till I saw you weeping tears
But you were my mother in my absentia

Even if you never knew which way I took
My lived reckless life you never saw
Still you have always prayed for me

Even when you could hardly imagine what I was
You still prayed to see me again
And even now still you are my mother

THE ARTS WORLD

Fellow brothers and sisters
Yes I mean you, my brother
And of course, why not, my sister

When I call upon brother and sister
I mean you and I in this world
Not any vulture around me

The real brave soldiers
Who have never fought rivalry
But revolutionary and were never acknowledged

Only sucked was their blood
By the self-proclaimed heroes
Hypocritical devils on this earth

Sucked will always be their blood
Entertaining the little peanuts
That a rat has left over

Have not only become entertainers
Or educators as we aim
But playing the so called "tatamachance"

Have become the entertained
With fake promises by fake persons
Who will never be mentioned

ONCE BOTTLED

Finally I heave this sigh of relief
To have received this talent
Enjoying the fresh oxygen

I am happier today than yesterday
I will be happier tomorrow than today
And sooner or later, I will rejoice

Standing free like flying
Right in front of all free doves
Symbolizing peace in their world

Sooner or later as I stand
You will as well stand
Celebrating victory

We will reap in the fields
Where our fore-parents ploughed
And never reaped

Have so long been bottled
Together with my talent
Thirst in water not allowed to drink

Exploring in exploitation
My prosperity tantalized in a tinted bottle
I have tilted down it until it broke

RIVAL TIME

It's now rival time
Not racial time
On a national torture

You see everyone in motion
And think they are on a mission
When they need promotion

It's the rival time
Succeeding the former racial time
With everyone rushing for survival

We all face a non-monopoly situation
A non-disorderly monopolization
With non-arrogance

The masked will soon be unmasked
Unmasked will regain passion
Either of the two has self-determination

I HAVE DREAMS

I dream dreams, born of dreams
My dreams are my own security
A fantasy full of divine mystery
Dreams of divinity and delight

When the sun shines I can dream
When the sun shines I can do
No mountain is too high too climb
No trouble too difficult to overcome
I dream dreams born of dreams

I refuse to be denied and refuse to be deprived
Simplicity is the ultimate form of sophistication
Assertiveness is not aggression
Insighting is never inciting
To be is to do and to do is to be
While ignorance belong to the arrogant

My realities, my dreams
My talent, my happiness and satisfaction
My satisfaction my recognition
My recognition my success
My success my dream
I dream dreams, born of dreams

I am done doing double task
My intention is your impression
I dream of my success
My success is my dream
My dream my success
I dream dreams, born of dreams

(A joint creation with Lerato Ditheko the best actress student, and all the Basa Tutorial Institute Drama participants of 2012).

ART ATTACKED

When I gained consciousness
Was when I felt the drowning
I could not be rescued from

I got infected sooner
At a very wrong time
To neither improvise nor experiment

Symptoms only showed out
When the virus was full blown
Yet no vaccine was found

To be distressed was not helping
As I already tilted with depression
No occupation could impress
But only arts embraced

Yelling out became useless
As I had got what I yearned for
I therefore yielded myself up
And lived positively

MY BLACK NATION

My fellow black nation
Living under oppression
Your being black
Is not being blind
But a blessing in disguise

It is high time you blend yourselves
Together with your oppressors
To block the oppression
And avoid blemishes
That intend spoiling your being black
For your being black is special

Being black does not mean being bloody minded
Let not yourself be blindfolded
But bloom and blossom
Blissful live black as you are
Because black is beautiful
Special and very important
Shine my black nation

GUYZ IN THE GHETTO

This comes as a special dedication
To all my guys living in the ghetto
The poor living in poverty
Yet not born to be

Ghetto style is a cool style
Rushing leads to crushing
Collusion occurs unconditional
The unrighteous will rush for wrong

Let us know we are poor
But not to be poor
Poor because of poverty
Poverty we live in

Let us not adjust
To negative civilization
Because of poverty
And let us not blame the innocent
For our failure not to try

Let us try and fail
And not fail to try
Let us not only be ghetto fabulous
By being ghetto scandalous
But be ghetto schedulers
With positivity in our poor communities

MERCIFUL VOICES

Almost every time in my lifetime
I hear those merciful voices
Crying out sorrowfully
For my solitary and soft soul
That now ceaselessly suffer

Telling me not to worry
About all the challenges
Assuring me of His guidance
Urging me not to abandon life
As I am not abandoned

Affirmatively assuring love and bliss
Prosperity that need my perseverance
Endurance that will be endowed
With eternity

Reviving my pulsated heart
Healing my desolation
Freeing me from slavery of thoughts
Ultimately restoring my hope
From all the unshunned feelings

MINUTE MULTI-MILLIONAIRE

Through this great realization
And the undergone research
The gone through experience
That pricked the unhealing wounds in my heart

I have no wonder why many die poor
Just as many have died
They will still die poor
When they do get economically rich

The big question stands between us
The minute multi-millionaires
We still need the knowledge
More that the riches we rush for

We must get rid of the bees
Buzzing only where it blossoms
Then disperse, leaving nothing on the stigma
Living the plant weary
And continue with their nomadic life

FEEL SO THREATENED

Creator of the universe created man in His image
Gave him the ability to think and rule
Gave him the power to be the hardworking
Striving not to surpass none other man

What then is the man thinking
Ruling over other men not himself
Wanting man to disciple his slavery
Aggressively drawing me closer

When I humble to make him my shepherd
He smashes my head to kill me
When I ask why he feels challenged
And live to become a watchdog against me

When I express my feelings
He fears my bravery and potentiality
Then despise and disguise
Instead of strengthening

When I am tranquil and accepting
Inferiority struck him most
Then try to shatter all my goals
And leaves me puzzled
Should I fake myself to make it?

LIQUOR, MY FRIENDLY ENEMY

Liquor, my friend
You have helped me escape reality
And sensibility to my burdened life
Even though you are cowardous sometimes

You have made me stop my necessary contemplations
Made me do non-necessities with uncertainty
You took gentle bites on me
Made me cowardous to myself

When I am weary
You have made me take a rest on you
When I am desolated and agitated
I get you next to me and relax
I drown my sorrows in you

You have managed my tranquility
Maximized my sociability
And multiplied my morality
You plea to my discontentment thoughts
Up until I get sober

You are a friend who multiplies my true and false friends
When my heart is dilapidated
My soul in agony
My head smashed with too many thoughts
You are indeed my friend

IN MY CURSED COLORS

Always dressed shabby in my cursed colors
Seen around now and again
The born nobleman
Often in agony and agitated
Embarking in people's grievances
Through inquisitiveness for the utmost
Discouraging dissatisfaction

Always seen in tatters and heartily tattered
The often traitored and tortured
Enduring loneliness and tragedy
For integrity and bravery
Often called attitude of no multitude tolerance
Undaunted man by no obstacles nor challenges

Still scruffy in these cursed colors
Is a man who strives not to surpass other men
But yearns to furthermost his goals
For those that strive to progress fairly
The gullible catch a glimpse of his tattered tatters
And shut the doors intending to shatter all his hopes

The nobleman will still compete non-with no man
But pursue superior performances
Conjures human endeavors
To endure for his achievements
And continue to make a step towards the next

DILAPIDATED HEART

Dip down the bottom of my dilapidated heart
The glinted glamorous light
Brought about gloom to my life
Its glamour gloomily left me

When I caught a glimpse of it
I gladly glided
Glibly bombarded with nice words
Because I was gladdened by its glamour
Moreover, by the glimmer of hope I had

While in no time now
My sensations
Have left me with no sensibility
But insanity and sorrow

When I sit and recall
Every thought become senseless
When I saunter down the streets
I am unconscious of the surroundings

When resting in bed looking up, the ceiling is surely
Optimistically chatting with friends
Make them too sententious to me
With all shun being my feelings

REVIVED AND DEPRIVED

Oh what a commemoration with futility
A victory with no success
Caught in a trapped velocity
Verged with unabridged big river

The positivity has now perversely turned
The vicious become victors
The prompted courageous cowarded
By the cowardous
The hypocrites sought to abuse
And pretended to be venturous
When stuck in a concrete jungle
Contrived and convinced for their own vintage

In despair and deceived by disguised faces
The innocent was caught up
Between revival and deprivation
With sabotage in hindrance to non-enormity
But fear of self-created storm
By a hypocritical fellow full of fear

FEARFUL MIND

The fearful mind of a guru
Makes the giant wonder
Why the grass is green
When it is the right springtime
When all plants are growing
Small or big
The leaves are young and new

The guru keeps forgetting
Winter is the only cold time
When we all shiver a lot
More than in any season
That may bring colds
Like the rain season
With its fear
The guru tries to be scare

LOVE PHOBIA

The first time I met you
Was like landing on another land
I was just so nervous
In a way I had never been
With some ever awful shivers

Talking to you in every single time
With those unrememberable words
Were double things I kept forgetting
With my heart beating very frantically
And you told me some awful words too

I mentioned I felt quite queer
From head down to toes
With no immune for the disease
I did not quite understand
What ailed me
And only you had the cure

But you called a nasty
Even looking so lazy
But crazy
Because of the uncommon fever
That love gave me

PERHAPS

Perhaps tomorrow
If it never comes
Perhaps tomorrow again

If not tomorrow
Perhaps
In some other time

Again if not
Perhaps in life
Perhaps always
And perhaps till death

LEAVING YOU, LIVE YOUR LIFE

With all that I have done to your life
I intended making you my wife
And gave you all my love
That made you to be alive
Out of all our lives
I did out of love

Without realizing I wasted my time
I tried to make you part of my life
Hoping that you'd be my wife
For the rest of my life
You took all my love
Even for the people I liked

Now the way I live
Is not how I wanted to live
You left me so lame
That I became so slim
And looking like no life

For that I decide to leave
You live your
Still I have my life led
We will meet in life
If we're all still alive
I loved you
But I have to leave
You live your life

OLD MAN CARES

The life of a very old man
Being the old and only one
Sitting in a very old chair
Chatting to his very old wife
While they themselves have wine
If not, VO Martell
Telling each other's dreams
Reminding themselves about their childhood dreams
During the days of their lives
Of the very old good days
That rolled swiftly during those old good times

The world changes
But their good life never changes
Even though it challenges
With a chain of choices
The old man cheers his wife
And cares for his family

Even when life threatens
He tightens his thoughts
And strengthens himself
While teasing his wife
Wiping her weeping tears
Calming and cunning same time
To shun her shocked sorrowful feelings
Yes, the old man cares

A BLACK AFRICAN FOOTPRINT

Here I stand in front of all of us
With only one visible label
Simple, the color of my skin
In a visionary mind
That will never be skinned

Allow me to mention this
I do not stand here as a mercenary
Nor a missile to attack
But as a missionary of my culture
The merit of my African being

Standing non-racially but promotionally
Proud of my being African and black
Call me a racist if you want
When I am not either
Instead, the ambassador of my people
And the Africanism

I stand with no technology
Only with tautology of my own culture
The tradition of a black African
Where stepped a black African
Printed is my African Culture
My pride and inheritance

Again, I stand not to repudiate other cultures
But reproduce and pronounce my rich African
The reputedly dying
Hence retaining to my people
Our Africanism and tradition

OUR CULTURE

Massive
Before venturing into our lives
Of non-velocity and visions
With non-veracity
Sophisticated and ventilated
On this modern version of life

Yesterday was not the same as today
Will never be the same as tomorrow
Yesterday, culture used to be our heritage
Our art descended from our ancestors
Parents were proud of our arts and culture

Today we have adjusted into Western civilization
Adopted too much into their cultures
Which we do not know their basics

It may have come from evolution of mankind
Now on revolution of different races
But our culture is our heritage

ARTS AVENUE

Somewhere in my City of Hellbrow
In my country Safa Safika
Lies the arts avenue
One of the dirtiest streets in town
With the greatest multitudes
Playing the dirtiest games ever
It is where mysteries and the mysterious are

It is where I am too
When I sought to have a better future
Seeking for greener pastures
And trying to pave my road to fame
I landed myself into shame
When poverty landed upon my figure
While futility struck my feelings
With great marginalization I could not imagine

Still sorely striving to make ends meet
Nurturing my talent
And make solid my vision and mission
Not conceding poverty to shatter my dreams
But linger-longing not longer
Up and down this arts avenue
In a revolutionary manner
On a mission with a vision
Sooner or later I will take off

The Tragedy in a Tangled Talented Mind

LionheART Publishing House

For all your publishing needs.

<u>Services include:</u>

Copyediting
Proofreading
Formatting
Cover Design and Creation
Book Trailers
Book Promotion Services

www.lionheartgalleries.co.uk
publishing@lionheartgalleries.co.uk
www.facebook.com/LionheartPublishing
@LionheartG

An imprint of LionheART Galleries

LionheART Publishing House

www.ingramcontent.com/pod-product-compliance
Lightning Source LLC
Chambersburg PA
CBHW071852020426
42331CB00007B/1974